GW01375590

10 + 1 QUESTIONS

You were too afraid to ask a Barista

Send questions, observations or threats to:
coffeegeekquestion@gmail.com

First published in 2016
First edition copyright © Kamil Kamieniecki

Designed by Stavros til01 Georgakopoulos
Cover photography credits to Stella Morais and Eduardo Cariglino
Printed and distributed independently by the author

All rights reserved.
No part of this book may be reproduced by any means, or transmitted, nor translated into a machine language, without the written permission of the publisher.

Condition of Sale
This book is sold subject to the condition that it shall not, by way of trade or otherwise, be lent, re-sold, hired out or otherwise circulated in any form of binding or cover other than that in which it is published and without a similar condition including this condition being imposed on the subsequent purchaser.

Dark Liquid School
43 Forburg Road
Stoke Newington
N16 6HP
London, UK

ISBN: 978-1-5262-0181-2

This book would not have been written without the help of Peter Theoklitou, Yannis Tsantoulis, Benjamin Alessandrini, Dale Harris, George Anagnostou, Kevin Van Der Ham, Stavros Georgakopoulos, Ankur Gulati and a few others who I will probably remember after it has gone to print and will feel very bad about it. Guys, this is a heart felt 'thank you'.

In memory of
Matthew David Gibson Baillie.

Prologue:

Good evening. Or, morning.

Throughout the years, while working in the coffee business, I have encountered so many questions from customers –or even myself– that it is no wonder coffee is perceived to be a complicated issue in many regards.

My initial struggle, was to find information that could address in a simple and efficient way these questions. What I soon realised, was that I could find answers to all these questions only because I was already working in the industry (hence, I knew where to look at for answers), or because I would dig so deep into the *information rabbit hole*, so that in the end, things would simply make sense. And this made me think, *what about the customers? Or, the simple coffee fans? Things must be alien to them. That is why they do not ask questions and try to educate themselves while ordering a drink*. Because there is pretentiousness in the air and things seem way too complicated. And this is the main reason i decided to write this book.

I hope many of the subjects that you will find in here, will shed some light on issues that might be puzzling you, or even give birth to more questions, which is the geeky part, the one we all love. Please, though, understand that this is only us scratching the surface of something very deep. If you wish to understand things in depth, may this be the starting point of a wonderful journey that people like me have embarked upon a while ago and still have not reached the end. Simply because there is no end; only the journey.

Enjoy.

-Can I please have a mocha
with vanilla syrup?
Could you please add
extra chocolate sprinkles
on top?
Skinny.
Please.

What is speciality coffee? What makes it better from the rest?

For starters I would like to address a simple question. The question that asks which spelling is correct: specialty or speciality? The answer is both. Speciality is American and speciality is the British spelling. Now, what that is...

When you open up a business that does coffee, you chose which path you want to take. A more mainstream approach which will give you a decent profit margin but a mediocre product, or a top-notch product with a smaller profit margin? If you chose to do speciality coffee then you need to follow two specific guidelines.

The first relates to the actual product. The coffee, the bean. It needs to be graded as speciality. What that means, is that the actual beans have been graded by people whose job is to judge and approve and grade coffee, these guys are called Quality Graders and they are the bad ass mothers. They will only include a coffee in the speciality batch if it scores more than 80 points (out of 100) and has no primary defects. If it scores less than that it can still be a decent coffee (i.e. commodity coffees) but obviously, as the grade decreases, the perceived quality drops accord. Coffee is cupped by individuals who have been appointed by an organisation called Coffee Quality Institute. When cupping, quality graders use a spread sheet in conjunction with the SCAA's (Speciality Coffee Association of America) guidelines, and judge the beans according to these specifications. Speciality coffee represents about 3% of the global market. So, no, you can not make as much money from it as a high-street coffee chain makes from their 'secret blend', because the price that you will buy speciality coffee is higher than the commodity coffee's price tag.

The second set of considerations when making speciality coffee is to follow the rules, protocols, guidelines that the Speciality Coffee Association of America or Europe (SCAA/SCAE) has put down for us; the coffee nerds.
The main idea was: we've got all these hundreds of nutcases out there playing with coffee and fighting with each other about what is right and what is wrong, but there's no referee in the game, so it's time to lay down some ground rules. And so they did. Now, if you, as an entrepreneur/barista/shop owner follow these guidelines is another matter. But if you want to make the most out of your expensive bean, then you would better follow the guidelines. Guidelines include using coffee beans graded as speciality, water filtration analysis, machine maintenance, milk temperatures, sizes of cups and dozens of other issues you will enjoy (or not) working on. There is loads of other things that the SCAA does as well which you will find very interesting but that's for another time.

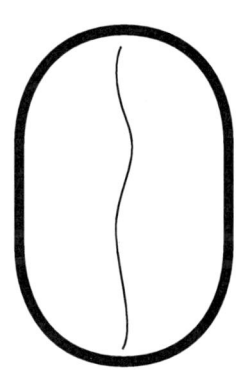

Coffee Bean

–Hello there,
can I...
have 'a'...
uhm...
flat w...
uhm no,...
I'd like 'a'

- OMG, next please!

02

Is the tap water filtered
or unfiltered
in speciality
coffee shops?

Filtered. Always and for everything that comes in contact with coffee. There are two reasons for that. First, the taste of the drink and second the health of our machines. Lots of things have been going on lately about water chemistry, and progress has been made on its effects in coffee. Yet, there is still much to be learnt, so exciting times ahead.

Most speciality coffee places that take seriously what they do measure their water. We –professionals who work in this type of sector– have a little tool called Refractometer or TDS meter (TDS not to be confused with STD in any way). Water is measured in parts per million (PPM). This is a way to describe dilute solutions in chemistry and SCAA guidelines ask us to keep this number between 75 to 250 ppm. A mini research will show you that keeping it roughly around 100 will make your coffee taste better as at that volume the flavours will be more sweet, clear and juicy.

Another reason to use filtered water is to keep the machine in good condition and reduce the need for maintenance. You see, if we used tap water through our equipment, it would build up scale in just a few months, and finally it would stop working since tap water has high concentrations of magnesium, calcium, carbonate and sulphate (among other chemicals).

Tip of the day: if you are brewing coffee at home, it is better to use bottled water, especially one that has a PH of 7. PH is the measure of how acidic or alkaline an aqueous solution is. It starts from 0.0 (acidic) and goes up to 14.0 (alkaline). What we call 'pure water' has a PH of 7 (to be super geeky I will say 6.81 at 37 Celsius degrees but let's stick with 7 to simplify things) and you can find quite a few bottled waters in the market in that range. And one useless piece of info is that your urine has a PH of 6, so if you would like to add a bit of acidity to your coffee give it a try.

Please, don't.

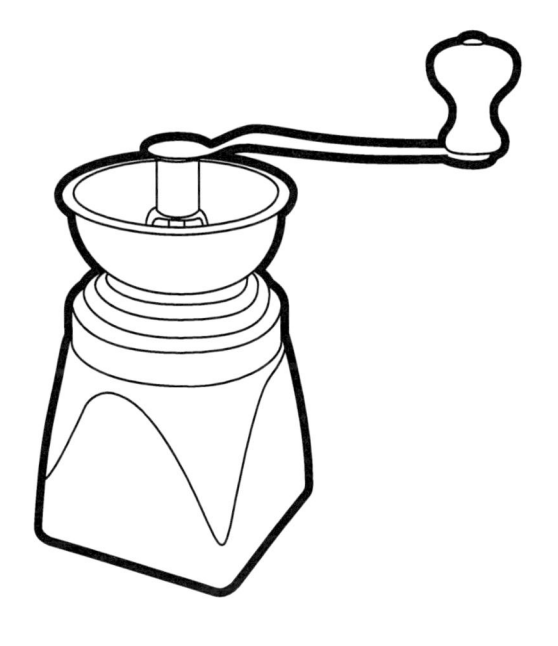

Hand Grinder

*−Can I have a triple shot
skinny macchiato,
with hazelnut syrup
and one sugar please?*

– Yes sure, would you like me to chuck a strawberry brownie into it as well? And some sprinkles?

Is caffeine a drug?
Is it addictive?

Yes, caffeine is classified as a drug. However, the chances of seeing you outside a tube station shaking and asking for coins because you are deprived of it, are quite low. Or, non-existent.

Our brain has these tiny receptors that rise up every morning and wait for a chemical to go and sit on them named adenosine. Adenosine is responsible for making us sleepy and tired and builds up during the day. Now, we have got this sneaky bugger called caffeine who happens to have the same shape as adenosine and once we have had this lovely cup of coffee, caffeine goes quickly and sits on the adenosine receptors and blocks its path. What our bodies have learnt to do though, is adapt, which means that our brain will grow more receptors each time, so that adenosine can have a spot to rest. Then you will decide to have more coffee because that one cup did nothing to you. And then you will get even more receptors growing, and even more adenosine, but you will fight it with even more caffeine, and . . . oh well . . . the war never ends.

We always suggest people not to overdo it with coffee consumption simply because it might cancel its effects since your body will get used to it and because big quantities can give you headaches, irritability, heart palpitations or less worrying symptoms like simple de-hydration.

Caffeine has the opposite effect on the body and brain to something called melatonin, which is regarded as having relaxing effects. If for any reason you have had too much coffee and need to sleep, you visit your local drug store and get a melatonin pill. Melatonin is found naturally in carrots or even purslanes. Now, just to make things clear –and avoid law suits– I do not recommend that you start taking pills because simply you have had too much coffee. Or, even start eating carrots in coffee shops. The first thing to avoid doing –after a big caffeine intake– is to avoid anything with sugar (even fruits) and drink plenty of water or some warmed up milk to help you relax. If you notice regular heart palpitations or uncomfortable body reactions to coffee please visit a doctor.

Another regular question us coffee geeks get, is why does a cappuccino provide a consumer with less of a kick than an espresso, even though they are both made from exactly the same amount of coffee? And the answer lies in the milk of the cappuccino. You see, milk, triggers the production of an amino acid in our body called Tryptophan, which has relaxing effects on our body (remember drinking warm milk before going to bed when you were a kid?), and when consumed with coffee, balances the effects of that 'kick'. Not that it de-creases the effect of caffeine, it just stabilises our reactions simply because we consume two products with a contrasting effect.

Porta Filter

—Morning,
Latte with two sugars please.

—Yes. Please.

-Uhm...
you'd like me
to put the sugar in for you?

-Really? Why?
Who am i? Your mother?

04

What is the difference between single origins and blends? What is best?

There is no such thing as best, or most tasty. If you are happy with how it tastes then "God bless". There is, however, a difference between qualities of beans (see first question) but let there be no confusion that there is one coffee out there that is simply the best.

A single origin bean is the one that comes from one country, and one specific farm. Sometimes we are even lucky enough to get our hands on packs that are labelled Micro Lots, which takes it even further as this coffee is from a specific part of the farm that at a specific time - or year - gave a tasting profile so unique that it had to be differentiated from the rest of the farm's harvest. Unfortunately, for commercial and promotional reasons, some companies use the term 'single origin' even if the coffee has come from different farms of one country and it might even be of different varietals. Long story short, if the coffee you bought is an actual single origin, it will indicate the farm of the country it comes from.

A blend is a combination of beans from all over the world (well, not ALL over the world, just from the growing regions) that a company or a roastery decided to put together and come up with a flavour profile that they were happy with. Now, there are two reasons why you would make a blend. One is financial and the second one is because of its taste.

Taste wise, when you serve single origin coffee you try to promote the flavours and aromas of the given farm and region. In some cases, however, it might be a little bit too much for some consumers as some countries produce too acidic coffees, or coffees for example with too earthy flavours. It all has to do with taste preferences, and the fact that employing highly trained staff who are able to create unique recipes for each bean is challenging and costly. For example, a Guatemalan coffee brewed as an espresso might taste great when extracted to 35ml through 18gr of coffee, but an Ethiopian might taste too acidic, therefore the recipe will need to be adjusted accordingly.

Although blending coffees is considered to be a tricky practise that requires skill by the roaster – and sometimes does not necessarily lead to a cheaper product – companies who are focused on a more mainstream clientele chose to go with that option.
A roasting company, may also use a cheaper coffee to fill a percentage of a coffee bag in order to drop its wholesale price.

Therefore, for all the above reasons, it is commercially less risky to go with the blend option.

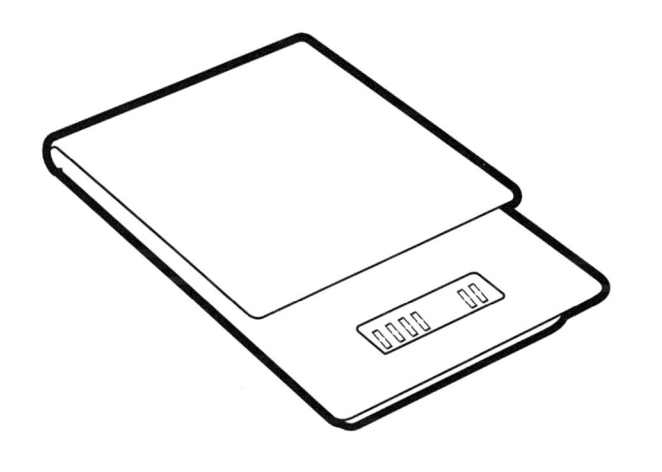

Scale

– *Hey there, besides the coffees from Kenya and Panama, do you do any Italian coffee? I love Italian coffee!*

– Uhm...
i have to be honest with you.
When Italians
start cultivating coffee,
Norway will be
the biggest banana exporter!

How many types of coffees are there? How can we tell what is good and what is bad?

Coffee is a plant that grows fruit. In the same way as an apple tree grows apples of all sizes, colours and shapes, same goes for coffee.

The four most popular coffee species are Arabica, Robusta, Excelsa and Liberica. Let us focus on the first two as these are the ones which are the most readily available and widely consumed.

Arabica species is the 'good' bean. All speciality coffee comes from Arabica beans. Robusta is perceived as its ugly little brother, who for some reason though, is always stronger than the pretty Arabica one. Here, we need to clear up the misunderstanding that Robusta is a 'brother' to Arabica, when Arabica is actually the 'son' of Robusta!

Speciality coffee uses Arabica varieties because of their flavour and aroma characteristics. Although Arabica coffee is more difficult to grow as it needs higher altitudes and it is not as resistant to bugs and diseases, it is the species we choose to work with for the above reasons. Robusta coffee is usually blended with some Arabica beans for commercial reasons (since Robusta usually costs less than Arabica) and used by some big chain brands who wish not to reveal where their coffee comes from. Robusta's flavour profile is that of a more bitter one, with a heavier body and much more caffeine content (1.7 – 4.0 % compared to Arabica's 0.8 – 1.4 %).

Now, just like it happens with apples, we start with one species but we get thousands of varieties/varietals. Depending on where the coffee was grown and under what conditions, it might have mutated throughout the years into a new varietal which will have its own unique flavour characteristics and even shape of plant/fruit. At this point, there are thousands of Arabica varieties throughout the world, though most of them are not used in modern markets, here is a small selection of the most popular ones:

- Bourbon (red, orange, yellow)
- Caturra
- Catuai
- Heirloom varietals
- Geisha
- Typica
- Maragogype
- Mundo novo
- Pacamara
- Pacas
- SL28
- SL34

Tamper

– Double X-presso please.

– A 'what'?!

How should someone taste coffee?

Good coffee does not taste bitter. In fact, coffee has even more flavour and aromatic compounds than wine. Such is the complexity of the flavour profile, that you should distinguish more sweet and sour flavours than actual bitterness.

Of course, this is us, talking about good quality beans that have been processed correctly, roasted well and prepared properly by your barista. If you go and ask for an espresso at your high street chain shop then all of the above does not apply since as we talked about earlier, these companies use blends that include vast amounts of Robusta beans, which, by nature are more bitter than Arabica beans. Also, their Baristas do not follow the most strict guidelines in coffee preparation.

When tasting coffee we always recommend you have it black. No sugar, no milk. So start with an espresso or a filter, and by filter we do not mean americano but V60 or Chemex. If you are not familiar with these types of brews then ask your local barista or do a quick web research.

When taking a sip, try to slurp, like a wine taster. Just make the most noise you can. This is to suck air inside the mouth and help release the aromas and flavours of your liquid and push them up to your nasal passage, it also helps spread the liquid on your pallet. Now, while tasting, try to distinguish the following: the acidity of your drink (which will hit the sides of your mouth and will remind you for example of lemons or green apples), the sweetness, which will be more noticeable at the front and might give you hints of all kinds of fruits or even chocolate, the body of the drink, meaning how syrupy it feels or how watery, and after swallowing, what we call the aftertaste. Is it pleasant? Is it bitter? How long does it last? While sipping, use your nasal passage as much as possible by exhaling air through your nose and analysing the aromas. Do you smell nuts, chocolate, cranberries? Remember that if your nose is stuffed up, it will be really difficult for you to do a proper tasting.

    If your coffee was well prepared and was of a speciality grade, you should not feel the need to add sugar to it as the coffee would already have unique characteristics and adding sugar would impose a different character to the flavour.

    The beauty of it is that with time you will be in a position to distinguish between origins, and maybe even varietals and become one of us weirdos who go 'Oh I'm a big fan of Brazilian coffees but I don't do Ethiopian, only maybe if they are of a natural process though . . . '

Jug

– Guys, I've got your drinks ready! Soya latte and a double espresso, thank you!

- *Thank you!
Oh, uhm...
which one's which?*

Why is it called americano? Why people confuse it with filter coffee?

As I am sure you will have noticed in American movies, when someone goes to a restaurant or one of those off-the-highway diners, they usually ask for just 'coffee' and the waitress brings them a percolator and pours coffee from it into their cups. Now, that coffee is made from a filter brewer, a bulk brew as we call it. Here is, how the confusion took place.

During the World War II, many Americans who stayed in Italy would visit a café and ask for coffee and as it was normal for an Italian barista, he would serve them espresso. Then the soldier would go "Hey champ, you're having a go here? I asked for coffee you mother...!" So what the Italians came up with was, pulling a double shot of espresso and then pouring it into a mug of hot water, and named it americano. Another way to make that would be to just let the shot of espresso run for a minute until it fills the cup (ouch!).

So at this point, both sides where happy. Though as the Americans called that a filter coffee (since that is what it was back home), it actually was not because it was brewed in a totally different way, but, the confusion had already taken place.

Something interesting that you should know about americano coffee though, is that it tastes more bitter than a double shot of espresso, even though an americano could come from that same espresso shot. Why is that?

The reason this happens, is that one of the liquids that form the espresso is natural oils. These oils coat your tongue and in a way, block the bitter tastes of the drink. Now, if you pour that very same shot in a cup of hot water you dilute the oils and cancel their effect on your sensory system, allowing some of the negative flavours that might exist to be revealed.

V 60

*–Can I have a mocha
with chocolate in it please?*

Why don't you make my latte as hot as it should be? Can I make frothy milk at home?

Just like with water, when it comes to milk, we could write a whole book about it and it would still need to be reviewed on a regular basis.

Milk has a natural sugar called lactose. Lactose is responsible for the sweet taste you get once you heat your milk up to a specific temperature. Most speciality coffee shops heat the milk between 60 – 71 degrees Celsius and there are three main reasons for that. First, you get to taste the best sweetness of the milk at that temperature which compliments your coffee, anything hotter than that, will reveal what we like to call 'burnt' flavours. Second, after a specific temperature you denature the proteins of the milk that stabilize your foam and it becomes very hard to create a uniform texture. Last but not least, if the milk gets too hot, your taste buds will not be able to distinguish any of the flavours and aromas we would like you to have experienced. Long story short, this is why speciality shops heat the milk less than your high-street coffee chains. Because we care about you, because you are amazing.

Now, about the home frothing thing. Suppose you do not have an espresso machine, there is one more way to trick your friends or impress a girl/boy with your latte art skills. You will need a French press, or press filter or cafetiere as some people call it. Heat up some milk, pour it into the French press, and then, for about 5-10 seconds move rapidly the plunge up and down. This will introduce air into your milk and create a type of foam. You can remove the plunger – or lid – and transfer the milk to a pouring milk jug. From there you can pour it into your coffee and try to create hearts, tulips, rosettas or dragons with the face of your soul mate. Wait, what?

Cafetiere or French Press

Middle aged lady slowly comes close to a barista and in a secretive voice asks:

**-Uhm...
do you have...
Wee-Fee...?**

Which coffee is the strongest? Does tea have more caffeine than coffee?

Tea has more caffeine than coffee. You did not expect that. Did you? But... there is always a 'but'!

Only by volume. By this we mean that using the same amount of coffee beans and tea leaves in a drink, will yield different levels of caffeine in it. For example, if you use three grams of tea leaves, you will extract a decent amount of caffeine into your beverage. For coffee though, you would need something between 14-18 grams of coffee beans in order to create a double shot drink. In speciality, we usually use about 3 grams for teas, and on average 18 grams for a cup of coffee. Now imagine using 18 grams of tea leaves into your drink. The answer would probably be 'hospital'. No, just kidding, you probably would not be able to even drink that.

Now, as to which coffee is the strongest I am afraid there is no specific and universal answer to that. But for start I would encourage you to speak to your barista and ask if they do double shots as a standard for espresso based drinks. Which means that any coffee on the menu that is made with an espresso machine, will have the same quantity of caffeine (as long as all shots are extracted in the same way/recipe). However, it is worth mentioning that a flat white will taste stronger than a latte since in a flat white, you will have less milk than a latte. Same goes for a long black (or short black) tasting stronger than an americano, even though they both have a double shot, a long black would have less water diluting the coffee, therefore taste stronger. One more area we need to consider when it comes to caffeine content (and this is without taking into account other forms of brews like Aeropress, Cold Brew, French press etc.) would be the filter type of brew. By filter, in this case we refer to a V60, or any hand poured filter coffee, where we usually use slightly less coffee than a double shot of espresso – 16 grams for filter to 18 grams for espresso – but as a drink is higher on the list of caffeine dosage for the reasons that coffee is brewed for a longer time (3 minutes for filter to 35 seconds, give or take, for espresso) and the drink is much longer in mls than that of a double espresso (270-300mls for filter to 30-35mls for espresso). So, provided you will enjoy the whole cup of your nicely made filter, you will receive a stronger dosage of a kick.

        Just to make the subject of caffeine content even more complicated, keep in mind that a coffee's strength will vary, depending on its species, varietal or even altitude level that the coffee was grown at. Yeah . . . tell me about it . . .

Timer

*A black americano please.
With skimmed milk.*

What is roasting? Does darker roast have more caffeine?

Beans, come unroasted, fresh and green, just like a regular plant/seed. In order to allow the coffee to release its flavours and aromas we need to roast it. In geeky terms, roasting is a process of manipulating the chemicals of the bean in order to get the gasses, acids, oils and sugars, among other things, that we want.

How roasting works is that every coffee has its own roasting style that suits its characteristics. A few years ago, there was an espresso roast (dark roast) for coffees that were to be used as espresso and a filter roast (lighter roast) for coffees that were to be used for filter brewing. In the world of speciality these rules do not apply as every coffee has its own character and the way to get the best out of every bean is to find that sweet spot we feel it allows it to shine. Meaning that a light roast, would be alright to be brewed as an espresso just because that would suit the specific type of bean.

There has been a confusion as to if darker roast has a higher caffeine content than lighter. To be honest with you, there is no clear answer to it as there has not been any official proof based on chemical analysis yet. One side will argue that because the bean gets smaller when roasted dark, you will need more beans for an 18gr. shot, therefore you will have more caffeine extracted from these 18gr as the caffeine content in a bean is not affected by the shrinking effect. On the other hand, we have people saying that as you roast coffee darker, you burn

some of the natural chemicals, including some of the caffeine, which would mean that your 18gr. shot would have less of it. No matter which side is right, the difference would be so small that probably this is the reason why no one has been bothered to take the issue into a lab.
One thing for sure is, that the darker roast will taste stronger. And by stronger we mean more persistent flavours/aftertaste. More burnt sugar and caramel characteristics than fruity and acidic notes. This happens, because like we said earlier, as you roast darker, you destroy one by one the chemicals in the coffee, and the last ones to be destroyed are the ones that give us some of these negative flavours and aromas.

      Maillard reactions, that happen during the roasting process are responsible for coffee's brown colour, bittersweet flavours and also aroma. For the sake of not overcomplicating things, just think of a steak being roasted. A roasted steak will get brown but remain juicy, then get darker and start losing its texture and in the end get burned. Maillard reactions take place only in roasting and not boiling, that is why your delicious beef stew is usually nice and soft no matter for how long you boil the meat.

Cup
(how exciting)

— Can I have a latte with that Guatemalan bean please?

— Thanks. Is it gonna taste like pineapple though? Cause it says at the bottom that it tastes like pineapple. Could you not put that in? I don't like pineapples.

- Yeah sure, good choice!

+1

Coffee is washed? How is it washed? With what?

1

Relax, we do not soap your coffee…

What you see on the speciality coffee bags is the process the coffee has been through before it arrives for roasting. The most popular processes for beans are either a natural process (dry), or a washed process (wet).

Coffee beans come in cherries. They look like little fruits hanging from plants, other times red, yellow or orange and of various sizes and shapes. In order to take the beans out of the cherries and give them an initial flavour characteristic we use a few different processes but here we will explain the two main ones we mentioned above.

The natural process involves collecting the cherries and placing them on large patios or raised beds at an outside space. Every now and then, they will be turned from the other side so that the sun sees it equally and no bacteria is formed. Then, with the use of a de-pulping machine, the coffee beans will get separated from the outer skin/fruit, get stored for 30 to 60 days and once the dry parchment is removed, shipped.

Now, in the washed process the cherries are moved into a floatation tank where they get separated from the unripe and other leaves/sticks. Then a de-pulping machine will push out the beans from the outer fruit. Once the bean is mostly parted from its layers, it gets placed in a fermentation tank, so that the natural sugars and alcohol that the mucilage of the bean includes, get broken down and removed from it naturally. The fourth step would be to wash the beans in tanks with water so that any mucilage left on the parchment is fully removed. Then, just like with natural process, the beans are placed out on patios to be dried, just this time without their cherries/outer layers. Once the beans reach the required amount of moisture (between 11%-12%), they are left to rest with their dry parchment for 30 to 60 days, which is then removed and shipped to us.

       These processes affect the flavour. The natural process gives us a more sweet coffee with good body and the washed process accents acidity and juiciness. Which process will be used for the coffee, is not always for the farm to choose. There are places in Ethiopia or Costa Rica for example, that do not have enough water supply in order to use the washed process and this is why they usually produce natural process coffees.

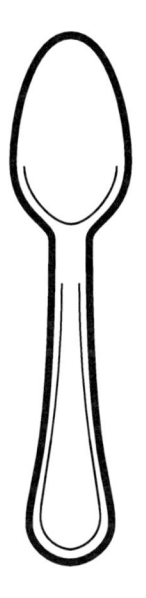

Spoon
(more excitement...)

Epilogue:

Walking into a speciality coffee shop may seem a bit intimidating at times. Seeing menus with all that information about different types of beans, varietals, flavour profiles and words like V60, Aeropress or whatever. You will be positively surprised, though, by how eager most of us are to answer any of your questions. Actually we look forward to educating people in what we call the 'third wave' of coffee culture. Please, do come forward and engage with us baristas, supervisors or floor staff. Through questions, you do not just educate yourself and evolve as a consumer, but you help us as well in further reflecting on what we might already know or even question our own knowledge.

Coffee culture has been growing rapidly during the past few years in many cities around the world. It has come to a stage where we use chemistry labs, scientists, apps and electronic equipment that seems way out of place, and we could not be happier about it. It is an exciting period to get into coffee, whether it is as a professional or as a consumer. There is just so much there for all of us to gain from.

And . . . cheers!

Kamil Kamieniecki has been working in the coffee industry since 2011 in London/UK. He has extensive experience in production, QC and training staff, both in commodity and speciality settings. When not working as a barista, or attending talks and cupping sessions, he plays drums in bands and travels all around the world.